Hypnotism and Mesmerism

By Annie Besant

Copyright © 2021 Lamp of Trismegistus. All rights reserved. No part of this publication may be reproduced or transmitted in any form or by any means, electronic or mechanical, including photocopying, recording, or by any information storage and retrieval system, without permission in writing from Lamp of Trismegistus. Reviewers may quote brief passages.

ISBN: 978-1-63118-587-8

Esoteric Classics

Other Books in this Series and Related Titles

The Religion of Theosophy by Bhagwan Das (978–1–63118–565–6)

Clairvoyance and Psychic Abilities by A Besant &c (978-1-63118-403-1)

The Feminine Occult by various authors (978-1-63118-711-7)

Rosicrucian Rules, Secret Signs, Codes and Symbols by various (978-1-63118-488-8)

An Outline of Theosophy by C W Leadbeater (978-1-63118-452-9)

Paracelsus, the Four Elements and Their Spirits by M P Hall (978-1-63118-400-0)

Essays on Ancient Magic by Helena P Blavatsky (978-1-63118-535-9)

Essays on the Esoteric Tradition of Karma by A Besant &c (978-1-63118-426-0)

The Use of Evil by Annie Besant (978-1-63118-532-8)

Occult Arts by William Q. Judge (978-1-63118-559-5)

The Alchemical Catechism of Paracelsus by Paracelsus (978-1-63118-513-7)

Alchemy in the Nineteenth Century by Helena P Blavatsky (978-1-63118-446-8)

Qabbalistic Teachings and the Tree of Life by M P Hall (978-1-63118-482-6)

The Historic, Mythic and Mystic Christ by Annie Besant (978–1–63118–533–5)

The Hidden Mysteries of Christianity by Annie Besant (978–1–63118–534–2)

The Brotherhood of Religions by Annie Besant (978–1–63118–563–2)

Kali the Mother by Sister Nivedita (978-1-63118-558-8)

Arcane Formulas or Mental Alchemy by W W Atkinson (978-1-63118-459-8)

The Machinery of the Mind by Dion Fortune (978-1-63118-451-2)

Vision of the Spirit by C. Jinarajadasa (978-1-63118-560-1)

The Leadbeater Reader: A Selection of Occult Essays (978-1-63118-483-3)

Audio versions are also available on Audible, Amazon and Apple

Other Books in this Series and Related Titles

Spirits of Various Kinds by Helena P Blavatsky (978–1–63118–586–1)

The Hidden Language of Symbolism by Annie Besant (978–1–63118–585–4)

Eastern Magic & Western Spiritualism by Henry S Olcott (978–1–63118–584–7)

Spiritual Progress and Practical Occultism by H P Blavatsky (978–1–63118–583–0)

Memory and Consciousness by Besant & Blavatsky (978–1–63118–582–3)

The Origin of Evil by Helena P Blavatsky (978–1–63118–581–6)

The Camp of Philosophy: Studies in Alchemy by Bloomfield (978–1–63118–580–9)

The Testaments of the Twelve Patriarchs (978–1–63118–579–3)

Occult or Exact Science? by Helena P Blavatsky (978–1–63118–578–6)

Occultism, Semi-Occultism & Pseudo Occultism by A Besant (978–1–63118–577–9)

The Fourth-Gospel and Synoptical Problem by G R S Mead (978–1–63118–576–2)

On the Bhagavad-Gita by T Subba Row &c (978–1–63118–575–5)

What Theosophy Does for Us by C W Leadbeater (978–1–63118–574–8)

Spiritual Life for Man by Annie Besant (978–1–63118–573–1)

The Mysteries by Annie Besant (978–1–63118–572–4)

Fundamental Ideas of Theosophy by Bhagwan Das (978–1–63118–571–7)

Dreams: What They Are and Caused by C W Leadbeater (978–1–63118–570–0)

Communication Between Different Worlds by Annie Besant (978–1–63118–569–4)

Animism, Magic and the Omnipotence of Thought by S Freud (978–1–63118–568–7)

Buddhism by F Otto Schrader (978–1–63118–567–0)

Death by W W Westcott (978–1–63118–566–3)

Audio versions are also available on Audible, Amazon and Apple

Table of Contents

Introduction...7

Hypnotism and Mesmerism

Note from Madame Blavatsky...9

Part 1...11

Part 2...26

Occultism is not the acquirement of powers, whether psychic or intellectual, though both are its servants. Neither is occultism the pursuit of happiness, as men understand the word; for the first step is sacrifice, the second, renunciation. Occultism is the science of life, the art of living.

INTRODUCTION

The word "esoteric" can be difficult to define. Esotericism in general can be seen less as a system of beliefs and more as a category, which encompasses numerous, different systems of beliefs. It's a bit of juxtaposition, since the word "esoteric" indicates something that few people know about, while the term itself broadly covers numerous philosophies, practices, areas of study and belief systems.

In a greater sense, Esotericism acts as a storehouse for secret knowledge, which is often considered ancient (by *tradition, if not by fact)*, passed down from generation to generation, in private. At various times in history, simply possessing the knowledge of some of these subjects, was considered illegal and a jailable offence, if discovered. This usually included such general topics as Alchemy, Pharmacology, Qabalah, Hermeticism, Occultism, Ceremonial Magic, Astrology, Divination, Rosicrucianism and so on. Collectively, these areas of study were often referred to as the esoteric sciences.

Sometimes, the outer garment of a subject isn't esoteric, while what is hidden beneath it, is. As an example, Freemasonry isn't necessarily esoteric by nature (at *least not anymore)*, but certain signs, passwords and handshakes given to the candidate during their initiation, are in fact, esoteric, in the sense that they are hidden from the general public.

Today, in the twenty-first century, such topics are readily available at bookstores across the country, and numerous mainsteam publishers offer beginners guides and coffee-table volumes on many of these subjects, intended for mass appeal. Books like *"The Secret"* have turned previously arcane topics into household knowledge. All that being the case, however, it isn't to say that there still aren't buried secrets to uncover, ancient wisdom being ignored and forgotten mysteries to be explored. In fact, it is often that we are only able to further our own studies by standing on the shoulders of these disappearing giants.

Lamp of Trismegistus is doing its part to help preserve humanity's esoteric history by making some of these classics available to those students who are seeking to unearth the knowledge of these ancient colossi.

So, be sure to check other titles from our *Esoteric Classics* series, as well as our *Occult Fiction, Theosophical Classics, Foundations of Freemasonry Series, Supernatural Fiction, Paranormal Research Series, Studies in Buddhism* and our *Christian Apocrypha Series.* You can also download the audio versions of most of these titles from Amazon, Apple or Audible, for learning on the go.

HYPNOTISM AND MESMERISM

NOTE

Mesmerism and hypnotism differ completely in their method. In hypnotism the nerve-ends of a sense organ are first fatigued, and then by continuance of the fatigue are temporarily paralysed; and the paralysis spreads inwards to the sense-centre in the brain, and a state of trance results. The fatigue is brought about by the use of some mechanical means, such as a revolving mirror, a disc, an electric light, *etc.*. A frequent repetition of this fatigue predisposes the patient to fall readily into a state of trance, and permanently weakens the sense-organs and the brain. When the Ego has left his dwelling, and the brain is thus rendered passive, it is easy for another person to impress ideas of action upon it, and the ideas will then be carried out by the patient, after coming out of trance, as though they were his own. In all such cases he is the mere passive agent of the hypnotizer.

The method of true mesmerism is entirely different. The mesmerizer throws out his own Auric Fluid..... through the etheric double, on his patient; he may thus, in the case of sickness, regularize the irregular vibrations of the sufferer or share with him his own life-force, thereby increasing his vitality. For nerve-atrophy there is no agent so curative as this, and the shrivelling cell may clairvoyantly be seen to swell up under the flow of the life-current. The prânic current flows most readily from the tips of the fingers, and through the eyes; passes should be made along the nerves from the centre to circumference, with a sharp shake of the fingers away from the patient and the operator, at the end of the pass. The hands should be washed before and after the operation and it should never be undertaken unless the mind is quiet and health is strong. The loss of vitality should be made good by standing in the sun, with as little clothing on as possible, breathing deeply and slowly, and retaining breath between inspiration and exhalation as long as is convenient, *i.e.,* not long enough to cause any struggle or gasping. Five minutes of this should restore the prânic balance.

"H.P.B."

PART 1

For many years the scientific world in Germany and France has been stirred to its depths by the experiments in hypnotism made by some of the leading physicians of each country. Both from the philosophical and the practical sides it has been realized that the strange power which formed the subject of investigation was one of supreme importance as its bearing on the constitution and conduct of man. Many of the records of alleged feats by witches and wizards of the middle ages — regarded by the nineteenth century as the mere drivel of superstitious ignorance — paled their ineffectual fires before the wonders of the new experimenters, while visions of the saints received startling pendants from the Salpêtrière. In Germany, the State, with characteristic promptitude, appears to have armed itself against the practical dangers which threaten to assail society, with a law that forbids unqualified persons to practise hypnotism. On the other hand, the Materialists, recognizing by a true intuition the fatal character of the new departure for the Materialist philosophy, assailed the experimenters with quite theological virulence, scoffing at their experiments and decrying their motives. The famous Dr. Ludwig Büchner — whose services alike to medicine and biology have been great — has vehemently attacked those of his compatriots who have entered the new path. In the last edition of his "Kraft und stoff" he speaks "of the legerdemain and claptrap of magnetisers, clairvoyants, thaumaturgists, spiritualists, hypnotists, and other jugglers." [*Force and Matter*, English translation, p. 338] Yet even he alludes to the hypnotic as a "highly interesting condition" [*Ibid.*, p. 346] and suggests that "it is probable that hypnotism accounts for much that occurs at exhibitions of animal magnetism". He remarks, indeed that "the whole effect is brought about by strictly natural causes", a statement with which Theosophists, at least, will not quarrel.

Hypnotism — derived from υπνος, sleep — obtained its name from its resemblance to somnambulism; in most respects the hypnotic resembles the mesmeric or magnetic trance, but differs from it in this, that suggestions made to a person under hypnotism are carried out when the hypnotic state has apparently passed away, and not during the trance as in ordinary mesmerism. Everyone who has seen the mesmerized person obey the mesmerizer, accept his fictions as facts, and perform at his bidding acts of the most startling absurdity. But when the patient recovers his senses, the spell is broken. Not so with hypnotism. The patient opens his eyes, walks about, goes away, performs the ordinary duties of life, but obeys with undeviating regularity the impulse communicated by the hypnotizer, imagining all the time that he is acting as a free agent while he is the bond-slave of another's will. There can be little doubt, however, that all these phenomena are but phases of the same condition. Hypnotism is a new name, not a new thing, its differentia being but extensions of the old "mesmerism".

From the time of Mesmer onwards attention has from time to time been directed to the curious phenomena obtained by mesmeric passes, fixity of gaze, *etc.*, but M.M. Binet and Féré, in their work on *Le Magnetisme Animal*, [The references in the text are to the English translation issued under the title "Animal Magnetism."] give to Dr. James braid, a Manchester surgeon, the credit of being "the initiator of the scientific study of animal magnetism" [p. 67]. "Magnetism and hypnotism", say these authors, "are fundamentally synonymous terms, but the first connotes a certain number of complex and extraordinary phenomena, which have always compromised the cause of these fruitful studies. The term hypnotism is exclusively applied to a definite nervous state, observable under certain conditions, subject to general rules, produced by human and in no sense mysterious processes, and based on modifications of the functions of the patient's nervous system. Thus it appears that hypnotism has arisen from animal magnetism, just as the physico-medical sciences arose from the occult sciences of the "Middle Ages". Braid found that many persons could hypnotize themselves by gazing fixedly at an object a little above the head in such a position that they eyes, when fixed on it squinted — or, to put the matter in a more dignified fashion, in such a position as induced convergent and superior strabismus. the fixation of the attention was also necessary, and Braid considers that the insensibility of idiots to hypnotism arises from their incapacity for fixed attention [pp. 69, 70]. At the Salpêtrière, Dr. Charcot and his pupils, dealing with hysterical patients, [*Études cliniques sur la grande Hystérie*, par le Docteur Paul Richer] found that catalepsy could be produced by sudden sounds or vivid light, and that the patient could be made to pass from the cataleptic to the somnambulic or lucid hypnotic condition by friction on the scalp, pressure on the eyeballs, and other methods. Speaking generally, Dr, Richer states that stimulants "which produce a sudden shock to the nervous system and cause sleep by marked hysterical symptoms, such as twitching of the limbs, movements of swallowing, a little foam on the lips, pharyngeal murmur, *etc.*, give rise to the nervous condition termed lethargy; while those which gently impress the nervous system and cause none of the hysterical symptoms to which I have alluded, produce a sleep which comes on progressively and without shock, the characteristics of which, differing from those of lethargy, belong to the special nervous state known under the name of somnambulic" [p. 519], or hypnotic. The ticking of a watch, the steady gaze of the Doctor, magnetic passes, a verbal command, *etc.*, will throw many subjects into a hypnotic trance.

The condition of a hypnotized person may vary from insensibility to accute sensitiveness. The body may be rendered insensitive to pain, so that critical operations may be performed without the use of a material anaesthetic, and a number of such cases are on record. On the other hand hypnotization often produces extreme hyperaesthesia. Binet and Féré say: "In somnambulism (hypnotism) the senses are not merely awake, but quickened to an extraordinary degree. Subjects feel the cold produced by breathing from the mouth at a distance of several yards (Braid). Weber's compasses applied to the skin, produce a two-fold sensation with a deviation of 3° in regions where, during the waking state, it would be necessary to give the instrument a deviation of 18° (Berger). The activity of the sense of sight is sometimes so great that the range of sight may be doubled, as well as sharpness of vision. The sense of smell may be developed so that the subject is able to discover by its aid the fragments of a visiting card which had been given him to smell before it was torn up (Taguet). The hearing is so acute that a conversation carried on, on the floor below may be overheard (Azam). These are interesting facts. We are still without any collective work on the subject, of which it would be easy to make regular study, with the methods of investigation we have at our disposal. More careful observations of the state of the memory have been made, but this state has only been studied as it has been found during the same hyper-excitability as the other organs of the senses (Binet and Féré, pp. 134,135).

Memory may, indeed, be rendered extraordinary vivid under hypnotism. A poem read to a hypnotized person was repeated by her correctly; awake she had forgotten it, but on again being hypnotized she repeated it. A patient recalled the exact *menu* of her dinner a week ago, though awake she could only remember those of a day or two ago. Another gave correctly and without hesitation the name of a doctor whom she had seen in childhood, although in her waking condition she, after some doubt, only recalled the fact that he had been a physician in a children's hospital.

Many of the purely physical results are interesting in themselves, but to the Theosophist, less suggestive than those which pass into the psychical realm. Contractures can be caused, and be transferred from one side to another, by a magnet. A limb can be rendered rigid, or can be paralysed, and so on. An extremely curious experiment is the tracing of some words on the arm of a hypnotized subject with a blunt probe; the doctor then issued the following order: "This afternoon, at four o'clock, you will go to sleep, and blood will then issue from your arm, on the lines which I have now traced". The subject fell asleep at the hour named, the letters then appeared on his left arm, and marked in relief, and of a bright red colour, which contrasted with the general paleness of the skin, and there were even minute drops of blood in several places. There was absolutely nothing to be seen on the right and paralysed side (the patient was affected with hemiplagia and hemianaesthesia). Mabille subsequently heard the same patient, in a spontaneous attack of hysteria, command his arm to bleed, and soon afterwards a cutaneous haemorrhage just described was displayed. These strange phenomena recall, and also explain, the bleeding stigmata which have been repeatedly observed in the subjects of religious ecstasy, who have pictured to themselves the passion of Christ. Charcot and his pupils at the Salpêtrière have often produced the effect of burns on the skin of hypnotized subjects by means of suggestion. The idea of the burn does not take effect immediately, but after the lapse of some hours (Binet and Féré, pp. 198-199). The bearing of these experiments on the supposed miraculous impressions of the sacred stigmata is obvious, and offers one more of the many illustrations which show that the best way to eradicate superstition is not to deny the phenomena on which it rests, many of which are real, but to explain to them, and to prove that they can be produced by natural means.

Muscular contractions of the limbs produce corresponding changes in the face, normally expressive of the feelings suggested by the artificially produced attitude. Richer states "A tragic attitude impresses sternness on the face, and the brows contract. On the other hand, if the two open hands are carried to the mouth, as in the act of blowing a kiss, a smile immediately appears on the lips. In this case the reaction of gesture on physiognomy is very remarkable and is produced with great exactitude....One can thus infinitely vary the attitudes. Ecstasy, prayer, humility, sadness, anger, fear, can be represented. It is, indeed, startling to see how invariably a simple change in the position of the hands reacts on the features. If the open hand is stretched outwards, the facial expression is calm and benevolent, and changes to a smile if the arm is raised and the tips of the fingers brought to the mouth. But without altering the attitude of the arms, it suffices to close the subject's hands to see the benevolence give place to severity, which soon becomes anger if the clenching of the fist is increased. This phenomena may be unilateral. If the fist is clenched on one side and carried forward as in menace, the corresponding brow only is contracted. So if only one open hand is brought to the mouth, the smile will appear only on one side of the face. The two different attitudes may be simultaneously impressed on the two sides of the body, and each half of the face will reflect the corresponding expression". (p. 669).

It is possible that these muscular contractions may give rise to no corresponding emotions, although it seems *prima facie* probable that where the emotions constantly find expression in gestures, the gestures should, in their turn, arouse the emotions. Yet it may be that the link is merely between muscle and muscle, and that the continual co-ordination results in a purely automatic action. We will, therefore, pass to phenomena in which the psyche is involved, and see what strange tricks can be played with it by the experimenter in hypnotism.

The lower senses of touch and taste and smell can be played with at will. A hypnotized patient, told that a bird had placed itself on her knee, stroked and caressed it (Richter, p. 645). "If a hallucinatory object, such as a lamp shade, is put into the subject's hands, and he is told to press it, he experiences a sensation of resistance and is unable to bring his hands together". (Binet and Féré page 213). Colocynth placed on the tongue is not tasted, odours are not smelt (Richter, p. 660). In the automatic state contact with familiar objects brings up the action constantly associated with them; given soap and water a patient will steadfastly wash her hands; given a match she will strike it, but is unconscious of pain if the flame touches her; given a probing pin, she will plunge into her hand; given a book, she will begin to read it fluently and, when the book is turned upside down, continue to read it aloud in the reversed position (Richter, pp. 693, 696). This automatic stage can be made to pass into the somnambulic, where the will is dominated, but where intelligence survives.

But it is when we come to the more intellectual sense of vision that we meet the most surprising phenomena. On a piece of white paper a white card was placed, and an imaginary line was drawn round this card, with a blunt pointer, without touching the paper, the patient being told that the line was being drawn. When she awoke she was given the blank piece of paper, and she saw on it the rectangle which had *not* been traced; asked to fold the paper along the line she saw, she folded it exactly so that it was just covered by the card when the latter was placed on it (Richter, p. 723). A patient was told that she saw a black circle; on waking she looked about, rubbed her eyes, and on being questioned complained that she saw a black circle in whichever direction she turned her eyes, and that it was extremely annoying (*ibid.*). A portrait was said to exist on a piece of blank cardboard; when the card was reversed, the portrait was reversed with it, and it disappeared when the other side of the cardboard was shown, although the changes of position were made out of sight of the patient (Binet and Féré, p. 224). Such a portrait is visible to the patient through an opera glass, and is magnified or diminished like a real object. Again, a patient, Bar — , was told that Dr. Charcot was present, and although he was not there she addressed him, told to listen to the music, she heard an imaginary concert; told that a number of children were present, she made gestures of taking them in her arms and kissing them, described the colour of their hair and eyes; while another patient complained that their play irritated her, and that the noise they made was intolerable.

More complex visions can be made to pass before the eyes; suggest to a patient that Paradise lies open before her, and she will see angels, and saints, the Virgin, and so on, the details of the vision varying with the richness of imagination of the patient. Sometimes it is the devil whose presence is suggested, and the most vivid fear and anger are expressed. Surely we have here the key to the visions of ecstatic nuns; the fixed gaze at the crucifix with upward turned eyes is the very position for self- hypnotization; the matter of the visions is suggested by the pressure of the dominant idea; while the certitude of the patients as to the reality of the visions would be complete.

Yet more curious are the phenomena connected with the rendering of an object or a person invisible by suggestion. Ten similar cards were shown to a hypnotized subject, and she was told that she could not see one of them. When she was awakened that card remained invisible; and similar results were obtained with keys, thermometers, and other objects. (Richter, p. 729). To another was said "You will not see M. X.", and on waking M. X. was invisible to her. "We once suggested to a hypnotic subject that she would cease to see F — , but would continue to hear his voice. On awakening the subject heard the voice of an invisible person, and looked about the room to discover the cause of this singular phenomenon, asking us about it with some uneasiness. We said, jestingly, 'F — is dead, and it is his ghost which speaks to you'. The subject is intelligent, and in her normal state she would probably have taken the jest at its true values; but she was dominated by the suggestion of anaesthesia, and readily adopted the explanation. When F — spoke again he said that he had died the night before, and that his body had been taken to the post-mortem room. The subject clasped her hands with a sad expression, and asked when he was to be buried, and she wished to be present at the religious service. 'Poor young man!' she said; 'he was not a bad man.' F—, wishing to see how farther credulity would go, uttered groans and complained of the autopsy of his body which was going on. The scene then became tragic, for the emotion of the subject caused her to fall backwards in an incipient attack of hysteria, which we promptly arrested." (Binet and Féré, p. 312,313). The most suggestive experiment was one in which F — was rendered invisible; the subject was then awakened, an on enquiring for F — was told that he had left the room. She was then told that she might retire, and went towards the door against which F — had placed himself. Unable to see him she came in contact with him, and on a second experiment to reach the door, became alarmed at the incomprehensible resistance and refused to again go near it. A hat was placed on his head, and "words cannot express" the subjects surprise, since it appeared to her that the hat was suspended in the air. Her surprise was at its height when F — took off the hat and saluted her with it several times; she saw the hat without any support, describing curves in the air. F — then put on a cloak, and she saw the cloak moving and assuming the form of a person. "It is", she said, "like a hollow puppet". A number of other experiments were tried with her, leaving no doubt that she was completely unconscious of F — 's presence (Binet and Féré, pp. 306-308).

In another class of experiments the subject's personality was changed. "On one occasion we told X — that she had become M.F. —, and after some resistance she accepted the suggestion. On awaking she was unable to see M. F —, who was present; she imitated his manner, and made the gesture of putting both her hands in her pockets of an imaginary hospital apron. From time to time she would put her hand to her lip as if to smooth her moustache, and looked about her with assurance. But she said nothing. We asked her whether she was acquainted with X — . She hesitated for a moment, and then replied, with a contemptuous shrug of the shoulders: "Oh yes, a hysterical patient. What do you think of her? She is not too wise."' (*ibid.*, p. 215, 216) Another patient personated in succession a peasant woman, an actress, a general, an archbishop, a nun, speaking appropriately in each character (Richter, pp. 729, 730).

There is another class of phenomena which opens up serious dangers of a practical nature. A suggestion made to a hypnotized subject may be carried out when the subject is awake, either immediately, or days or months afterwards, and this obedience is blind to consequences and to every consideration of right or wrong. We have a personality which is the puppet of another's will. Dr. Richter remarks: "In the latter state (cataleptic) the subject is an automaton, without conscience or spontaneity, only moving under the impulse of sensorial stimuli coming from without. The stimulus alone matters, and not the person who supplies it. The personality of the operator is indifferent. All the responses are of the nature of reflex actions, without any participation of the intellectual activity other than such as may be necessary for their production. The somnambulist, on the other hand is no longer a simple machine. He is the slave of the will of another, the veritable *subject* of the operator. His automatism consists in servitude and obedience. But certain consciousness exists other than that of the waking state. A new personality is created, which may give rise to those strange phenomena described under the name of duplication of consciousness or of personality. There is really a somnambulic Ego while there is no cataleptic Ego" (p 789).

It is in this somnambulic stage that occur the phenomena now to be considered. A hypnotized subject is required to steal some object; sometimes she resists, but insistance generally overcomes this resistance; only in a few cases has it been found impossible to conquer it. On awaking, the patient watches her opportunity and performs the theft and here comes in the curious fact, that the subject shows cunning and intelligence in carrying out the suggestion. One patient, told to steal the handkerchief of a certain person, presently feigned dizziness, and staggering against the person stole the handkerchief. In another case, the subject suddenly asked the owner of the handkerchief what he had in his hand, and stole it as he, in surprise, looked at his hand. Another, told, to poison X — with a glass of water, offered it with the remark that it was a hot day. "If Z — is armed with a paper-knife and ordered to kill X — she says, 'Why should I do it ? He has done me no arm'. But if the experimenter insists this slight scruple may be overcome, and she soon says: ' If it must be done, I will do it'. On awaking she regards X — with a perfidious smile, looks about her, and suddenly strikes him with the supposed dagger". The patient will find reasons to excuse her acts; one who had struck a man with a pasteboard knife under suggestion was asked why she killed him. "She looked at him fixedly for a moment, and then replied with an expression of ferocity, 'He was an old villain, and wished to insult me'" (Binet and Féré, pp. 286-291).

Without further accumulating these phenomena let us consider whether any, and if any, what explanation of them is possible.

And first from the standpoint of Materialism. It is possible to explain on a materialistic hypothesis the muscular contractions and co-ordinations, and the automatic actions succeeding contact with familiar articles. But even in the automatic stage, explanation is lacking of the fluent reading of a reversed book by an uneducated person. It is, however, in the phenomena of memory, of vision of the non-existent, of inhibited vision, that materialistic explanation seems to me to be impossible.

Memory is the faculty which receives the impress of our experiences, and preserves them; many of these impressions fade, and we say we have forgotten. Yet it is clear that these impressions may be revived. They are, therefore, not destroyed, but they are so faint that they sink below the threshold of consciousness, and so no longer form a part of its normal content. If thought be but a "mode of motion", memory must be similarly regarded; but it is not possible to conceive that each impression of our past life, recorded in consciousness, is still vibrating in some group of brain cells, only so feebly that it does not rise above the threshold. For these same cells are continually being thrown into new groupings for new vibrations, and these cannot all co-exist, and the fainter ones be capable of receiving fresh impulse which may so intensify their motion as to again raise them into consciousness. Now if these vibrations = memory, if we have only matter in motion, we know the law of dynamics sufficiently well to say that if a body be set vibrating, and new forces successively brought to act upon it and set up new vibrations, there will not be in that body the co-existence of each separate set of vibrations successively impressed upon it, but it will vibrate in a way differing from each single set, and compounded of all. So that memory, as a mode of motion, would not give us a record of the past, but would present us with a new story, the resultant of all those past vibrations, and this would be ever changing, as fresh impressions, causing new vibrations, came in to modify the resultant of the old. On the other hand, let us suppose a conscious Ego, retaining knowledge of all its past experiences, but only able to impress such of them on the organ of consciousness as the laws of the material organism permit, the threshold of consciousness dividing what it can thus impress from what it cannot; that threshold would vary with the material conditions of the moment, rising and falling with the state of the organism, and what we call memory would be the content of the material consciousness, bounded by the threshold at any given instant. Now, under hypnotization an extraordinary revival of the past occurs, and impressions long since faded come out clear-cut on the tablet of memory. Is it not a possible hypothesis that the process of hypnotization causes a shifting of the threshold of consciousness, and so brings into sight what is always there but is normally concealed? The existence of the Ego is posited by Theosophy, and it seems to me that the phenomena of hypnotization require it.

How can the Materialist explain the vision of non-existent things? We know what are the mechanical conditions of vision in the animal body; the rays reflected from the object, the blows of the ethereal waves on the retina, the vibrating nerve-cells, the optic centre — the perception belongs to the world of mind. But in seeing the invisible we have the perception, but with none of the steps that normally lead up to it; the suggestion of the hypnotizer awakens the perception, and the mind creates its own object of sense to respond to it. Again, it must be the perceptive power, not the sense channel, which is paralysed when objects and persons become invisible. Take the case of F — and his cloak; certain rays from the body of F — struck the retina of the patient, but no perception followed; for the cloak to be seen normally, the rays from it must traverse exactly the same line as those from his body, impinge on the same retinal cells, throw into vibration the same nervous cord, and so be perceived. If the inhibition were of the nerve elements, the rays from the cloak would be stopped like those from the body round which it was wrapped. The inhibition was not of nerve, but of mind; the operator had entered the subject world of the patient and had laid his hand on the faculty, not on the instrument. If perception be only the result of the vibrating cells, how comes it then that cells may vibrate and the result be absent? That in two cases the vibration may be equally set up, the same cells be in motion, and yet that perception follows the one vibration and not the other? A still further complication arises when the cloak is seen, though the body is interposed between it and the organ of vision. If perception result from cell-vibration, how can perception arise when no cell-vibration is set up?

But it seems that it is not only active perceptive faculty that the operator may bring under his control: he may lay hold of the will and compel the patient to acts, and so become the master of his personality. A terrible power, yet one can no longer be regarded as doubtful, and which recalls old-world stories of "possession", throwing on them a new and lurid light. How many of the tales of magic powers, which changed people's characters and drove them in obedience to the will of the "magician", are now explicable as hypnotic effects ? How often may the "evil eye" have caused injury by deliberate suggestion, as Charcot thus caused a burn ? I have often thought that there must have been a basis of fact underlying the widespread belief in witchcraft; and the possession of hypnotizing power, aided by the exaggerations of fear and credulity, would amply suffice to account for it. The general belief in evil spirits would lead to the ascription of the results to their agency, and the very ignorance of the nature of their own power by the "magicians" would foster the notion of supernatural interference.

The study of hypnotism drives us, if we would remain within the realm of natural law, of causation, into the belief that the mind is not the mere outcome of physical motion, however closely the two may be here normally related. That while the brain is "the organ of mind" on this plane, it is literally the organ and not the mind; and that it is possible, so to speak, to get behind the organ and seize upon the mind itself, dethroning the individuality assuming usurped control. On this hypothesis results of the experiments become intelligible, and we can dimly trace the *modus operandi*.

Theosophists may well utilize this new departure in science to gain a hearing for their own luminous philosophy, for the Western World cannot turn a deaf ear to the testimony of its own experts, and the experiments of those very experts force on the thought the impossibility of the mind and the will being the mere result of molecular vibration. Once carry a thoughtful Materialist so far, and he will be bound to go farther, and thus the very triumph of Materialistic science shall lead to the downfall of its philosophy.

PART 2

I - THE HISTORY

The attention of the scientific world in France and in Germany has long been directed to the curious phenomena which are classed as "hypnotic", and for years past experiments of the most searching character have been carried on by experts, notably at the Salpêtrière and in Nancy. In Germany, Heidenhain, one of the most eminent of German physiologists, has, since 1880, been investigating these phenomena, attracted thereto by the experiments of Carl Hansen, a Dane, the gentleman who in October last founded a Hypnotic Society in London, for the systematic study and use of Hypnotism. The phenomena are interesting, not only as being curious in themselves, and as promising to place in the hands of the physician a useful therapeutic agent , but also the light they throw on the psychical constitution of man, and on those subtle problems of life and mind which occupy the attention of the accutest thinkers of our time.

There can be no doubt, in the light of our present knowledge, that many of the "miraculous" cures credited to prophet and saint were the results of magnetic power; that the ecstasy of the saint is reproduced in the hypnotic trance; that witches and wizards may be rivalled by the mesmerizer. Much that was obscure is now illuminated, and the Salpêtrière patient explains the sybil and the seeress. We see prophecies, visions, possessions, the evil eye, magic control, all reproduced under conditions which render possible careful scrutiny and deliberate investigation.

The scope of hypnotism will, however, be poorly understood if we confine ourselves to the rigid experimentation of the French doctors. Valuable as is their work, placing hypnotism among the experimental sciences on a basis that none can challenge, we shall only understand its bearing by studying it from a standpoint that renders visible a wider horizon, and enables us to see it in relation to its historical evolution, as well as in its most modern presentment.

The soothing and curative power that lies in the human touch was known long ere the resemblance of some of its properties to those of the magnet gave rise to the name of Animal Magnetism. Solon (B.C. 637-558) speaks of the fury of disease being soothed by the gentle stroking of the hand, [Apud Stobaeum. Translated in Stanley's *History of Philosophy*, 1666] and in China the origin of the practice of curing diseases by the laying on of hands is lost in antiquity. Celsus records the fact that Asclepiades, the Greek "father of physic", "practised light friction, as a means of inducing sleep in phrensy and insanity; and, what is more remarkable, he says that by too much friction there was a danger of inducing lethargy". [*Somnolism and Psychism*, By J. W. Haddock, M.D., 1851, p. 7]. The Chaldean priests, the Parsīs, the Hindus, and other civilized people of antiquity, also practised cure by touch. There can be little doubt that this custom is alluded to in 2 Kings v, 11, where Naaman is represented as saying that he thought the Jewish prophet would "strike his hand over the place and recover the leper". The Egyptian sculptures show figures in magnetic positions, and the habit of taking to the sick cloths impregnated with a holy person is often met with in antiquity, and is spoken of in Acts xix, 12. The cures wrought by Vespasian at Alexandria, as recorded by Suetonius and Tacitus, were obviously magnetic, and the idea of the curative properties of the "King's touch" was but an inheritance from the time when the priestly functions attached to the royal office carried with them this healing power.

Nor was this use of human magnetism for the cure of diseases the only kind of magnetic phenomenon known to the ancients. Hippocrates, Aristotle, Galen, and other classical authors mention somnambulism, a state which may supervene naturally or be artificially induced, and is, in either case, a phenomenon now included under "hypnotism". Nor can there be much doubt as to the nature of the utterances of the sacred virgins in pagan temples. Of these Dr. Haddock says:

"From what is known of the practices, the long vigils and fastings, and the peculiar attitudes and manners of the sybils, there can be little doubt that by various means, kept secret from the multitude, a condition similar if not identical with the higher mesmeric, or *psychic* state, as it is proposed to call it, was induced; and that the sybils and utterers of oracles were, at times, really clairvoyant and in a state of trance. Saint Justin said 'that the sybils spoke many great things with justice and with truth, and *that when the instinct which animated them ceased to exist, they lost the recollection of all they had declared*'. It will be seen in the sequel that this is so strikingly in accordance with the mesmeric sleep or trance as to leave scarcely a doubt of its identity with it". [ibid. pp. 6. 7]

It is not definitely known when the properties of magnetized iron and steel were first discovered, the Chinese claiming to be the first to use the compass, but it is certain that the use of the magnet for curative purposes can point to a respectable antiquity. Paracelsus (A.D. 1493-1541) seems to have been the first, among Westerns at least, to ascribe magnetism to the human body, and to suggest the use of this human magnetism for the cure of disease; in his time magnets must have been used for this purpose, as we can judge not only from his expression of "human magnetism". but also from a work by Cardan, dated 1584, in which "there is an account of an experiment in anaesthesia, produced by the magnet", and it is stated that "it was then customary to magnetise rings, which were worn round the neck or the arm, in order to cure nervous diseases. [*Animal Magnetism*, by Binet and Féré. English Translation, 1888, p. 2]

Pomponatius (A. D. 1462-1525) had already pointed to the fact, which he speaks of as generally acknowledged, that some persons "gifted with the faculty of curing certain diseases, in virtue of an emanation from themselves which by the power of the will and imagination they are able to direct to the sick", [*Human Magnetism*, by W. Newnham, 1845, pp. 149, 150] "When those who are endowed with this faculty", says Pomponatius, "operate by employing the force of the imagination and the will, this force affects their blood and their spirits, which produce the intended effects, by means of an evaporation thrown outwards". [Quoted in *Isis Revelata*, by J. C. Colquhoun, 1836, vol i. p. 152] He considers that health may be communicated to a sick person, as disease may be communicated to a healthy one; and he alleges that matter, the elements themselves can be made subject to man by this magnetic force. In 1621 the celebrated Van Helmont (A. D. 1577-1644) published in Paris a remarkable work on *The Magnetic Cure of Wounds*, in which he defended magnetism as a curative agent, as against a Jesuit, Father Robert, who had maintained that certain cures were the work of the devil. "Magnetism", he writes, "is a universal agent; there is nothing new in it but the name; and it is a paradox only to those who are disposed to ridicule everything, and who ascribe to the influence of Satan all those phenomena which they cannot explain". He defines magnetism as "that occult influence which bodies exert over each other at a distance, whether by attraction or by repulsion", and considers that it acts through a fluid, the *Magnale Magnum*, an ethereal spirit which penetrates all bodies, and in the human frame is found in the blood, and is directed by the will. Man can so use it as to affect objects at a distance, and the strength of his impulsion depends on the energy and concentration of his volition. "This magical power lies dormant in man". So thoroughly convinced was Van Helmont of the reality of the magnetic force, that when the plague was raging at Brussels, he went thither to tend the sick. [See Isis Revelata, vol i, pp. 154-161] Many other authors wrote on the same lines during the seventeenth century, as Sir Kenelm Digby, in 1660, William Maxwell, 1679, and Robert Fludd. A remarkable quotation from a work published in 1673 by Sebastian Wirdig, is given by Mr. Colquhoun: "*Totus mundus constat et positus est in magnetismo; omnes sublunarium vicissitudines fiunt per magnetismum; vita conservatur magnetismo; interitus omnium rerurrm fiunt per magnetismum*". [*ibid.*, p. 150].

In 1889, Dr. Buck writes, in words that are wellnigh an echo of the seventeenth century philosopher: "We thus discern an underlying substance everywhere diffused, of great tenuity, permeating all things as the common basis of matter and force. This substance, with its characteristic polarizing tendency, and its universal diffusibility, outwardly displayed in atoms of the elements and in all objective phenomenal nature, is magnetism". [*A Study of Man,* by J. D. Buck. M.D., 1889, p. 31]

One of the most remarkable of the practical magnetizers of the seventeenth century was an Irish gentleman, named Valentine Greatrakes, who published an autobiographical sketch in 1666. Among his patients were the philosopher Cudworth and the astronomer Flamsteed, while Robert Boyle, President of the Royal Society, bears witness to the reality of his cures. Dr. George Rust, Bishop of Derry, writes as follows on what he himself saw, and his testimony is confirmed by members of the Royal Society, physicians, and others, who carefully examined into the alleged facts:

"I was three weeks together with him at my Lord Conway's, and saw him I think, lay his hands upon a thousand persons; and really there is something in it more than ordinary; but I am convinced it is not miraculous. I have seen pains strangely fly before his hands, till he hath chased them out of the body — dimness cleared and deafness cured by his touch; twenty persons, at several times, in fits of the falling sickness, were in two or three minutes brought to themselves, so as to tell where their pain was; and then he hath pursued it till he hath drawn it out at some extreme part; running sores of the king's evil dried up, and kernels brought to a suppuration by his hand; grievous sores of many months' date in a few days healed; obstructions and stoppings removed; cancerous knots in the breast dissolved, etc.."

The Bishop says further that the cures often took some time, and that patients often relapsed, while with others he could do nothing. His method was placing his hand on the affected part and stroking lightly from above downwards. The Royal Society considered that there was "a sanative influence in Mr. Greatrakes's body", and in a book which contains an article on the cures by Robert Boyle, is a remarkable cure of leprosy by " stroaking " by Greatrakes. [*Isis Revelata*, Vol. 1, pp. 203 to 207. See also Newnham's *Human Magnetism*, pp. 150, 151, and *Somnolism and Psychism*, pp. 8, 9]

In the eighteenth century John Joseph Gassner (born 1727) performed a number of cures, chiefly among patients suffering from epilepsy and other nervous complaints; a full account may be read in the German *Archiv für den Thierschen Magnetismus*, published at Leipzig.

From this rough sketch it will be seen when the man was born who was destined to give his name to this little-understood natural force, its existence had long been known, and it had been largely utilized. Anthony Mesmer (1734-1815) was born, some say at Weiler Germany, some, at Mersburg, in Switzerland, and while still young went to Vienna to study medicine. He did not take his doctor's degree until 1766, when he chose for his subject "*The influence of the Planets on the Human Body*", following Paracelsus in the theory that the planets influenced the human body through a subtle magnetic fluid. A Jesuit professor of Astronomy at Vienna, named Hehl, drew his attention to the loadstone as a curative agent, and Mesmer and Hehl together performed a number of experiments with magnetized steel plates. Some jealousy arose between them, apparently from Mesmer having discovered that "magnetic passes", movements of the hand from above downwards, much increased the value of the steel plates; what is certain is that Mesmer and Hehl fell out, and that Mesmer's proceedings so roused against him the Medical Faculty of Vienna that he was obliged to leave that city. He visited various towns, performing many cures in the hospitals and elsewhere, and after a varied experience came to the conclusion that the human body could produce effects similar to those produced by the magnet, and that "animal magnetism" was a powerful curative agent. About this time a man named Perkins, in England, patented for the cure of disease some "metallic tractors", which appear to have resembled the steel plates of Mesmer and Hehl; Perkins, however, did not grasp the luminous idea of Mesmer, that the curative power lay in the human body, and his discovery was discredited when Drs. Haygarth and Falconer produced with wooden tractors results similar to those produced by his metallic ones, [*Somnolism and Psychism*, pp. 9, 10] Mesmer, who had hold of the right principle, proceeded with his cures, and in 1778 arrived in Paris, whither his fame had proceeded him. He published in 1779 a pamphlet, in which he laid down his theory of animal magnetism, claiming that his "system would furnish fresh knowledge of the nature of fire and light, as well as of the theory of attraction, of flux and reflux magnet and electricity". "This principle can cure nervous diseases directly and others indirectly. By its aid the physician is enlightened as to the use of drugs; he perfects their action, provokes and directs at his will salutary crises, so as to completely master them". He summarized his twenty-seven propositions, many of which are recognized as true today, however startling they may have appeared to be to the science of the eighteenth century. The human body, he alleged, showed polarity — a fruitful idea, destined to have great results — and animal magnetism could be communicated to living and non-living agents, and operate from afar. Mesmer's first convert was Dr. D'Eslon, but doctors for the most part were bitterly hostile, and the Medical Faculty of Paris suspended Dr. D Eslon and denounced Mesmer and all his works, finally, in 1784, prohibiting the practice of animal magnetism by doctors under penalty of expulsion.

Despite this official excommunication, Mesmer had the bad taste to continue performing cures, and Paris, palpitating with new ideas, intoxicated with new liberty, went wellnigh mad over him. Fashionable society thronged his consulting room and fought for admission at his doors. Unfortunately Mesmer was not strong enough to master his own popularity, and lent himself to follies which brought discredit on his really great powers. Clad in purple silk, he wandered through the crowd of patients, amid soft music, in carefully subdued light, touching one with a metallic rod, another with the hand, provoking and controlling passionate excitement.

The patients were seated round a *baquet*, or trough, the contents of which set up a magnetic current; they were mostly dilettante, hysterical, credulous men and women of the court, in search new excitement. What wonder that such a crowd, dominated by the handsome presence and undoubtedly strong magnetic powers of the marvellous doctor, with the expectation of the wonderful ensuring its own realization, with the hysterical contagion to which a crowd is always liable, what wonder that convulsive crises were provoked, and scandalous scenes enacted?

Outside Paris, numerous "Harmonic Societies" were established, the members of which magnetized the sick poor gratuitously, and communicated to each other the noteworthy facts which occurred within their experience. [See *Isis Revelata*, Vol. i, pp. 238, 239. In this learned work is given a very full account of Mesmer, and the reader who desires to investigate the whole question of Animal Magnetism can find no more useful treatise, as it is crowded with references to the literature of the subject in ancient and modern times] At last it was felt that it was necessary to institute a careful inquiry into the whole subject, and Louis XVI, in 1784 issued a mandate to the Medical Faculty of Paris, desiring them to appoint commissioners and draw up a report. Two Commissions were appointed, one of members of the Academy of Sciences, including such men as Franklin, Bailly, Lavoisier, and Guillotin; the other of members of the Society of Physicians, among whom De Jussieu was the most famous. These Commissions reported against Mesmer, considering that his cures were due to the imagination of the patients, and that his system was injurious to morality. Attention was drawn in a special report to the details of the system. "The magnetiser generally keeps the patient's knees enclosed in his own", "the hand is laid on the hypochondriac region" and other sensitive parts of the body, and thus crises were provoked of a hysterical nature, detrimental to moral dignity and self-control. "Imagination, imitation, touches, such are the real causes of the effects attributed to animal magnetism. The methods of magnetism being dangerous, it follows that all public treatment in which magnetic practices are used must, in the long run, have the most lamentable results". But among these eminent men one of the most eminent dissented from the report presented by his Commission, and, while combating the theory of magnetism, refused to refer to imagination all the strange phenomena he watched with the trained observation of a naturalist. Of this dissident, De Jussieu, Dr. Paul Richer says:

"A faithful and accurate observer, he noted facts that had escaped the attention of the commissioners, or that they had voluntarily neglected. These facts are not beyond criticism, and moreover they are insufficient as the foundation of a theory, be it what it may. But it is not the less true that De Jussieu is the one savant who suspected that among all the phenomena, more or less strange and incoherent, then put to the debit and credit of animal magnetism, there were some in which the unknown was lying hidden, worthy of profound examination, and meriting something better than disdain or a simple non- acceptance". [*La Nouvelle Revue*, August, 1882. "*Magnétisme Animal et Hypnotisme*". par Paul Richer]

The insight of De Jussieu was to be justified by the future. It may be noted that Cuvier (1769 to 1832), who was in 1800 appointed Professor of Natural Philosophy in the *Collège de France*, later endorsed De Jussieu rather than his colleagues. In the second volume of his *Anatomie Comparée* he writes:

"I must confess that it is very difficult to distinguish the effect of the imagination of the patient from the physical effect produced by the operator. The effects, however, which produced upon persons already insensible before the commencement of the operation, those which take place in others after the operation has deprived them of sensibility, and those which are manifested by animals, do not permit us to doubt that the proximity of two animated bodies, in certain positions and with certain motions, has a real effect, independently of all participation of the imagination of one of them. It seems sufficiently evident, too, that these effects are owing to some sort of communication which is established between their nervous systems". [Quoted in *Isis Revelata*, Vol. 1, p. 74]

The belief in Animal Magnetism, which was now spoken of as Mesmerism, was not, however, to be crushed out by the unfavourable reports of the Commissions. As Mr. Colquhoun well says, the facts "almost daily disclosed were much too numerous, too unambiguous, and too firmly established, to be overthrown even by the united force of learning, prejudice, ingenuity, ridicule, invective, and persecution". In Germany, Lavater, in 1787, drew to it the attention of the medical world, and it has since steadily flourished there, and has given birth to a widespread scientific literature. In France, despite the Revolution its study proceeded, although Mesmer left the country, [Mesmer died in 1815, at Mersburg, on the Lake of Constance deeply beloved of the poor, to whose treatment he consecrated his powers in his later years] and three distinct schools of magnetism were established: that of Mesmer, proceeding by touches, friction, and pressure, use of the *baquet*, of magnetized water and plates applied to the stomach; a treatment provocative of violent convulsions and crises; that of Barbarin, which disregarded physical means and relied on the will of the operator and the most celebrated of all, that of Marquis Chastenet de Puysegur, a pupil of Mesmer, who took for his motto "Croyez et veuillez", and used magnetic passes without contact. De Puysegur practised chiefly on peasants of his vicinity, and worked a large number of cures, full accounts of which may be read in his published works. [In the third edition, 1820, of his *"Mémoires pour servir à l'histoire et a l'établissement du Magnétisme Animal"* I find no less than eight works advertised as from his pen. The "Mémoires" has for stamp a heartsease, surrounded by rays and ringed with the words, "Thought moves matter.."] It is to De Puysegur that we owe the first description of the magnetic trance, or lucid somnambulism, a discovery since so fruitful in results. A young peasant, named Victor, was suffering an affection of the chest, and was magnetised by De Puysegur, who thus describes the case:

"What was my surprise to see, in seven minutes, this man fall into a tranquil sleep in my arms, without convulsions or pains! I hastened the crisis, a proceeding that caused some giddiness; he spoke aloud on matters of business. When it seemed to me that his thoughts must affect him unpleasantly, I stopped them, and sought to inspire merrier ones; this did not require much effort, and he became quite content, fancying that he was drawing for a prize, dancing at a fête, *etc*...... I encouraged these ideas in him, and thus obliged him to move actively in his chair, as though dancing to a tune which, by singing it *mentally*, I made him repeat out loud". [Mémoires, pp. 21, 22]

De Puysegur tells us of a peasant "the most stupid man in the countryside", who taught him methods of magnetizing when in the "clairvoyant" state, and relates how his patient, in the magnetic state, "was no longer stupid, scarce able to stumble through a sentence, but becomes a being I can hardly describe, to whom I need not speak, for he understands and answers me if I merely think in his presence". [*ibid.*, pp. 27-29. The student will find a large number of instructive cases in this work] This lucid somnambulic state, as it has since been termed, attracted general attention, and the popularity of De Puysegur rivalled that of Mesmer.

Gradually doctor after doctor in France experimented in Animal Magnetism, or Mesmerism, with varying results. In 1820, in consequence of the investigations of a young medical man, Dr. A. Bertrand, the hospitals were opened for experiments, and the student may read Baron Du Potet's large collection of experiences. He relates some remarkable cures wrought by himself; but the "unreliability" of the little-understood natural agent in different hands, and the prejudice of the medical profession, barred the way to its general adoption. [*Manuel de l'Étudiant Magnétiseur*, par Baron Du Potet, Quatrième Edition Paris, 1868] Experiments successfully performed by one person on one day, failed at the hands of another person on the next day, and, the conditions of success not yet being understood, the failure seemed inexplicable and discouragement supervened. It was forgotten that, in the investigation of every newly-discovered natural force, similar successes and failures occurred; and it was as rash to denounce Animal Magnetism as unreliable because beginners blundered, as to deny that electricity could be produced by friction because a machine working in a moisture-laden atmosphere threw off no sparks.

In 1825, however, *Animal Magnetism* had progressed so much that it again applied in Paris for scientific imprimatur, and after five years of patient investigation a Commission, named by the Academy of Medicine, reported strongly in its favour, and declared that "the Academy should encourage research into Animal Magnetism, as a very curious branch of psychology and natural history. [*Nouvelle Revue*, loc. cit., p. 593] But the reading of this report, presented by M. Husson, raised a storm; one doctor declared that the Academy was being entertained with miracles, and another, that if the alleged facts were true they would destroy half our physiological knowledge; so that, finally, the report was shelved. In 1837, another Commission, composed almost entirely of the opponents of magnetism, was appointed, and another report issued, this time, as was expected, in hostility; this report was adopted by the Academy, and was clinched by the offer of a prize of 3,000 francs by M. Burdin, to anyone who could read without using the eyes and in darkness. M. Pigeaire, a doctor of Montpelier, submitted his daughter, who was able to read with her eyes bandaged, when in the magnetic trance; a commission was thereupon appointed to examine this child, who had her eyes covered with cotton-wool, and then carefully bandaged; the judges appear to have been harsh, and to have distressed the sensitive, who was accustomed to use the tips of her fingers for reading, as do many somnambulists, and after much discussion the prize remained unawarded. M. Pigeaire then offered a prize of 30,000 francs to anyone, not in the magnetic trance, who could read, wearing his daughter's bandage, and this prize also remained unwon. It may be remarked that the tips of the fingers, the pit of the stomach, and the centre of the crown of the head, are used by somnambulists for reading; a book placed in contact with one of these parts of the body is fluently read.

So for as France was concerned, Animal Magnetism now remained under a cloud, but in England it made great progress. Dr. Abercrombie, Dr. Haddock, Dr. Elliott, and many others, investigated it, and in most cases practised it, and with remarkable success. But the founder of the modern school of "hypnotism" was Dr. Braid, a Manchester surgeon, who seeing some experiments performed by Lafontaine, a Swiss mesmerist, in 1841, and believing him to be fraudulent set himself to work to discover the supposed imposition. He, however, came to the conclusion that the incapacity of the mesmerised patient to open his eyes was a real incapacity, and he began to experiment upon his friends, with the view of producing a similar phenomenon. He found that this closing of the eyes could be brought about by a fixed gaze at an object placed slightly above the eyes, so that a convergent strabismus was induced. When the hypnotic state was thus obtained, he found that the patient could be readily influenced, and that, by placing him in given attitudes, the emotions normally expressed by these attitudes could be produced in him at will. He further discovered that the senses often become abnormally acute under hypnotism, and that hallucinations could be imposed on the subject by "suggestion", *i.e.*, that a direction to see something on awaking was followed by a hallucination when the subject came out of the trance condition. Since the time of Braid, the whole question has been studied in the most strictly scientific spirit, experiments have been performed under rigid test conditions, and hypnotism is no longer an alien in the scientific world, but an accepted denizen, well worthy of careful attention. The world-famous experiments of Charcot and his colleagues at the Salpêtrière, and those of Liébault at Nancy, have for ever rendered impossible the recurrence of the follies of 1784 and 1837. The revival of the study in France was due to the experiments of Azam, a Bordeaux surgeon, in 1850, and various works on it appeared up to the year 1866, when Liébault published the results of his investigations. In 1878, the Salpêtrière school first attracted public notice, and from that time forward scepticism has been replaced by study in the scientific world.

In the Salpêtrière every source of modern science has been utilized to shut out the possibility of fraud, and those who doubt the results, startled by their amazing character, will do well to study Dr. Paul Richer's monumental work, *Études Cliniques sur la Grande Hystérie, ou Hystero-Épilepsie*. It has been found by numerous experiments that the tracings obtained by attaching a tambour to the arm and a pneumatograph to the chest of a subject thrown into cataleptic state are wholly different from those obtained from a subject in the normal condition; for instance, while a strong man may simulate some forced position, and the eye of the observer may be unable to distinguish any difference between his attitude and that of a cataleptic patient placed in a similar attitude, yet the strain in his case will be made evident by the tracings obtained from him, which are wholly different from those obtained from the other. Thus the tracing of the respiration of a person in hypnotic catalepsy showed smoothly-rounded curves, while the tambour on the limb gave an absolutely straight line; on the other hand, the respiratory tracing from a man who imitated the attitude showed sudden dives jerks, becoming sharper and sharper as the moments passed, and the tracing from extended limb, at first fairly straight, showed muscular tremors increasing in violence as the strain was prolonged. By these rigid tests was fraud excluded, and the certainty of the abnormal state established.

There are many ways in which the object can be thrown into the magnetic trance, such as holding the hands and gazing fixedly into the eyes, making downward passes over the face and trunk, placing the thumb on the forehead while the fingers rest lightly on the crown of the head, *etc.*. At the Salpêtrière, the operators, dealing with hysterical patients, have generally thrown the subject into the rigid cataleptic state first, by a sudden noise, as a blow on a gong, the flash of the electric light, or other sudden sense- stimulus; a slower way is a continued slight stimulus, as looking upwards at a dark or bright object — as in Braid's experiments. The subject may be made to pass from this cataleptic into the lethargic state by further stimulus, and from this into the "hypnotic", or lucid somnambulic, by light friction of the scalp. The true hypnotic lethargy is distinguished from catalepsy once more by respiratory tracings, those obtained from a subject passing from lethargy into catalepsy showing the change in the most unmistakable way, while a further check has been secured by making tracings of the circulatory changes (by the of the plethysmograph and air-sphymograph), which are as marked as those of the respiration. [See on these tracings Binet and Féré's work quoted before pp. 120, 134, where a number of these tracings are given; and, for greater detail. P. Richer's Études, pp 337-355 and 757-768]

II - THE FACTS

As long ago as 1636 Daniel Schwenter hypnotized a cock by tying its legs together, and placing its beak at the end of a chalk line drawn along the ground, an experiment still frequently repeated with success; the tying of the legs is quite unnecessary, as the animal remains motionless if the beak be held on the line for a few moments. Experiments on animals are satisfactory in so far as the possibility of fraud is here excluded, but of course only physical phenomena can be obtained from them. One word of warning is advisable, however, to any who embark on this line of investigation, especially if they practise on the domestic cat or any of the canine race. There is a moment, just before success, when the animal is roused to rage — probably by terror — and will spring at the operator. Any start or blenching then means failure, and an ugly bite or scratch may be the result.

The facts of Animal Magnetism, for purposes of study, may be conveniently classed under three heads: 1. Its use as a therapeutic agent. 2. The exaltation under it of the physical senses and mental capacities. 3. The control of the subject by the operator.

1. *Its use as a therapeutic agent.* — The cures worked by Greatrakes, Mesmer, Du Potet and other mesmerizers have already been alluded to, and during the present century a vast number of cures have been affected. Dr. Haddock records a case of blindness cured by him. A little girl of seven began to exhibit symptoms of cerebral affection, with partial paralysis, and eventually became totally blind; the child was brought to him, and by him submitted to a clairvoyante, who attributed the blindness to the state of the roots of the optic nerve and the disordered condition of the nervous system. The child was mesmerized everyday, and at the end of three

weeks began to perceive light, improving gradually until she was able to read large print. This occurred at the close of the summer of 1849 and at the end of 1850 the child had regained her sight, but was somewhat short-sighted. [*Somnolism and Psychism*, pp. 159, 160] A famous case is that of Harriet Martineau, who has left a record of her own experience; she describes herself as reduced to the last state of weakness, "a life passed between bed and the sofa". All that medical skill could do was done, and she was continually dependent on opiates. She then put herself under mesmeric treatment, and "at the end of four months I was, as far as my own feelings could be any warrant, quite well". She describes her steady convalescence, "improved composure of nerve and spirits", and the help she found mesmerism to be in breaking off the use of opiates". [Quoted in Newnham's *Human Magnetism*, pp. 421-427] Dr. Inglis of Halifax, cured a girl, eleven years old, of epileptic fits, by daily inducing mesmeric sleep, [*ibid.*, pp. 139, 140] a form of sleep that is accompanied with marked recuperation of the bodily energies. Perhaps the most remarkable use of magnetism, under this head, is its employment as an anaesthetic. One of the most famous operations performed on a mesmerized patient is the removal of the breast of an elderly French lady, Madame Plantin, for cancer, in 1829. Madame Plantin's physician, Dr. Chapelain, was in the habit of mesmerizing her, and he found that she would placidly discuss the advisability of the proposed amputation when she was in the mesmeric trance, but shrank from it, when awake, with "the most intense anguish and apprehension". M. Jules Cloquet, an eminent surgeon of Paris, was chosen as operator, and found his patient in the mesmeric trance on his arrival. "She spoke calmly of the intended operation; removed her own dress to expose her bosom to the surgeon's knife; and during the operation, which lasted about a quarter of an hour, she conversed freely with the surgeon, and the physician, who was seated by her, supporting the arm on the diseased side, without exhibiting the slightest pain or consciousness of what was going on". She was kept under mesmerism for two days, and the wound began to heal in a healthy manner but the patient died fourteen days later from another disease. [*Somnolism and Hypnotism*, pp. 45, 46] In 1851 Broca and Follin mesmerized a woman to make an incision in an abscess, and Guerineau, of Poitiers, amputated the thigh of a hypnotized patient. [*Animal Magnetism*, by Binet and Féré, p. 77] It is obvious that this use of hypnotism might prove most serviceable in cases in which chloroform cannot be employed without danger to life.

Carl Hansen has used mesmerism for the cure of nervous diseases of all sorts, for destroying by suggestion rooted ideas amounting to mania, for calming the insane in fits fury, etc., *etc.*. In India, where climatic influences are most favourable to the production of mesmeric phenomena, and among the sensitive Hindus, Colonel Olcott has cured diseases literally by the hundred, paralysis, blindness, deafness, dumbness, rheumatism and so on. The use of clairvoyance in the diagnosis and cure of disease will be mentioned further on.

2. *The exaltation of the physical senses and mental capacities.* — This class of cases is full of instruction for the psychologist, for here, if anywhere, he can study mental phenomena apart from normal conditions, though if he insists on invariably connecting states of consciousness with cell-vibrations, he will find himself in parlous difficulties.

The quickening of the senses and of the mental capacities belongs to the lucid somnambulic condition, not to that of lethargy. Binet and Féré say:

"The state of the senses in hypnotic subjects ranges from anaesthesia to hyperaesthesia. During lethargy all the senses are suspended, with the occasional exception of the sense of hearing, which is sometimes retained, as it is in natural sleep. During catalepsy, the special senses are partially awake; the muscular sense, in particular, retains all its activity. Finally, in somnambulism the senses are not merely awake, but quickened to an all extraordinary degree. Subjects feel the cold produced by breathing from the mouth at a distance of several yards (Braid). Weber's compasses, applied to the skin, produce a two-fold sensation, with a deviation of 3 degrees, in regions where, during the waking state, it would be necessary to give the instruments deviation of 18 degrees (Berger). The activity of the senses of sight is sometimes so great that the range of sight may be doubled, as well as the sharpness of vision. The sense of smell may be developed so that the subject is able to discover by its aid the fragments of a visiting card which had been given to him to smell before it was torn up (Taguet). The hearing is so acute that conversation carried on the floor below, overheard". [*Animal Magnetism*, pp. 134.135]

Many of the extraordinary phenomena of clairvoyance appear to be directly related to this abnormal sensibility, the bounds of time and space being ultimately completely cast aside. A girl of seventeen, named Jane Rider, was very carefully observed by her medical attendant, Dr. Belden; he found — amid many other curious facts — that she could read and write with two wads of cotton-wool over her eyes, coming down to the middle of the cheek, in close contact with the nose, and closely bound with a large black handkerchief; thus blinded, she on one occasion wrote the words *Stiff Billy*, and then correctly dotted the i in each word; wrote *Springfield* under them, leaving out the I, and went back and put the missing letter in the right place. [Isis Revelata, vol. i, p.

377] Schelling, the German philosopher, relates a case he observed, in which a clairvoyante began to cry, and said that the death of a member of the family had taken place at a distance of 150 leagues. She added that the letter announcing the death was on its way. On awaking, she remembered nothing and was quite bright and cheerful, but when again hypnotized she again wept over the death. A week later, Schelling found her crying, with a letter beside her on the table, announcing the death, and on asking whether she had previously heard of his illness, she answered that she had heard no such news of him, and that the intelligence was quite unexpected. [*ibid.*, vol. i, pp. 89, 92] Similar stories, vouched by names of the highest character, may be found by the dozen in books dealing with these phenomena, so there is nothing unjustifiable in the statement of Schopenhauer: " Who at this day doubts the facts of animal magnetism and its clairvoyance, is not to be called sceptical, but ignorant". [*Versucht uber Geisterschen*]

A use of clairvoyance that has been too much neglected is its employment for the diagnosis of obscure forms of disease. The Madame Plantin alluded to above had a daughter, Madame Lagandré, who was a clairvoyante, and who visited her mother shortly before her death; she described the state of the right lung and heart, the stomach and liver, describing the right lung as being shrivelled up, compressed, and no longer breathing, and saying that there was water in the cavity of the heart. A post-mortem examination was conducted on Madame Plantin's body in the presence of Dr. Drousart, M. Moreau — secretary to the surgical section of the Royal Academy of Medicine, Paris — and Dr. Chapelain, by MM. Cloquet and Pailloux. The state of the organs was found to exactly bear out the somnambule's description. [See *Isis Revelata*, vol. ii. pp. 87-89; and *The Philosophy of Mysticism* by Du Prel, vol. 1, p. 236. A full account is given by Dr.

Haddock in *Somnolism and Psychism*, pp. 54-56] Dr. Haddock's somnambule, Emma, constantly diagnosed diseases for him, and indicated appropriate remedies, which were applied with great success. [*Somnolism and Psychism*, Chap. 7] Here, again, a mass of evidence is available for all who desire to further study the subject. Dr. Sprengel, Dr. Brandis, Dr. Georget, and other physicians equally eminent, have advocated the employment of somnambulists for the diagnosis of disease.

Passing from the senses to the more intellectual faculties, we find that the memory becomes, to an extraordinary degree, retentive under hypnotism: a poem was read over to a hypnotized subject and she was awakened; she could not remember it, but on being again hypnotized she repeated it correctly. At the Salpêtrière a hypnotized subject gave the menu of dinners she had eaten a week previously. A hypnotized girl, in Charcot's room, was asked the name of a man who entered the room, and at once answered, "M. Parrot". She was awakened and again questioned, but said she did not know him; at last, after looking at him for a long time, she said that she thought he was a physician at the *Enfants assistés* (as was the fact). It appeared that she had been a the Refuge when she was two years old, but had naturally forgotten the physician: hypnotized, her memory promptly recalled even his name. [Binet and Féré, pp. 136.137] Similarly, the general mental capacity quickened. The girl before mentioned, Jane Rider, blindfolded carefully, was asked to learn backgammon; she consented, knowing nothing of the game, learned it rapidly, and won the sixth game from an experienced player; awakened, she was asked to play, but said she had never seen the game, and she could not even set the men. [*Isis Revelata*, vol. i. pp.381, 382] Dr. Abercrombie gives a long account of a girl, whom he describes as "when awake, a dull, awkward girl, very slow in receiving any kind of instruction, though much care was bestowed upon her"; but, when in the somnambulic condition, "she often descanted with the utmost fluency and correctness on a variety of topics, both political and religious, the news of the day, the historical parts of Scripture, public characters, particularly the characters of members of the family and their visitors. In these discussions she showed the most wonderful discrimination, often combined with sarcasm, and astonishing powers of mimicry. Her language through the whole was fluent and correct, and her illustrations often forcible and even eloquent. She was fond of illustrating her subjects by what she called a fable, and in these her imagery was both appropriate and elegant". [*On the Intellectual Powers*, pp. 296 et seq. Quoted in *Isis Revelata*]

Such facts as these, which might be multiplied a hundredfold, should surely give pause to the materialist, who will have thought to be nothing more than the result of the vibration of brain-cells; and if it be objected that, numerous as they are, these cases are yet exceptional and abnormal, we may fitly reply with Herschell: "The perfect observer will have his eyes, as it were, opened that they may be struck at once with any occurrence which, according to received theories, ought not to happen, for these are the facts which serve as clues to new discoveries". [*Preliminary Discourse on the Study of Natural Philosophy*, Sec. 127]

3. *The control of the subject by the operator.* — Here we come to the very heart of our question: to the most marvellous facts, the most serious dangers, and the phenomena most luminous for psychological discovery. This control of the hypnotized person by the hypnotizer is absolute, complete; as Dr. Richer says, " The somnambulist .... is no longer a simple machine. He is the slave of the will of another, the veritable *subject* of the operator. His automatism consists in servitude and obedience". [*Études Cliniques*, p. 789]

Take first the senses. These can be so deceived as to sensate when there is no object of sensation, to remain passive when stimuli are applied. The patient is plunged in the hypnotic trance; he is told that he will see or not see, feel or not feel, a certain thing; he is then awakened, but the "suggestion" continues to dominate his intelligence, and, apparently acting freely, he blindly obeys. A hypnotized patient was told that a bird was on her knee, and on awaking she stroked and caressed it; [*ibid.*, p. 645] another was told that he had a lamp-shade placed between his hands, and on awaking he pressed his hands against the imaginary object, and could not bring them together; [Binet and Féré, p. 213] a card was placed on a sheet of white paper, and an imaginary line drawn round the card on the paper with a blunt pointer, the pointer not quite touching the paper; when the subject awoke, the blank paper was given to her, and she saw the rectangle which had *not* been traced on it, and, on request, she folded the paper along the lines she saw, folding it to the exact size of the card. [*Études Cliniques*, p. 723]

The reality of the hallucination is strikingly shown by an experiment in which the subject was told that there was a portrait on a piece of blank cardboard; when she awoke she saw the portrait, when the cardboard was turned round the portrait was reversed, and when the other side of the cardboard was shown nothing was seen, although these changes of position were made out of sight of the patient. [Binet and Féré, p. 224] Even more strange is it that such an imaginary portrait is seen magnified or diminished if looked at by the subject through an opera-glass. A patient was told that Dr. Charcot was present when he was absent, and on awaking she addressed him; while another, told that she could not see Dr. F., was unable to see him though in the room; she was given permission to leave the room, and Dr. F., placed himself in front of the door; she came in contact with him without seeing him, and after making a second attempt to reach the door became alarmed at a resistance in the air she could not understand, and refused to make any further effort; a hat placed on his head was seen by her as suspended in the air, and a cloak he put on moved about "like a hollow puppet". [*ibid.*, pp. 306-308] I have myself been rendered invisible in this way, with the quaintest of results.

Another class of experiments is the formation of hallucinatory complex visions. A patient was told that Paradise was before her, and she described the Virgin Mary, the saints and angels, it being noticed that the details of the vision in such cases varied with the belief and fancy of the subject. [*Études Cliniques*, pp. 669 and 790] Another was made to see the devil; "she drew herself up, anger in her face, in a superb pose of wrath and defiance. At the end of a few moments she uttered a piercing cry, and fled to the other end of the room". [*ibid.*, p. 699, note] Another, described as a "very respectable woman, the mother of a family and very pious", was made to assume in turns the characters of a peasant, an actress — a very free-spoken one — a general, and a priest. We have here the explanation of many of the visions of nuns and others in a highly excited nervous condition; the upward-turned and fixed gaze is the very one used by Braid for self-hypnotization, and the dominant idea would take the place of the suggestion.

Absolute physical lesion can be caused by suggestion. Charcot and his assistants have produced the physical effects of a burn by suggesting to a hypnotized patient that she has burned herself; a doctor traced some words with a blunt probe on the arm of a hypnotized subject, and told him that at four o'clock blood would come out on the lines traced; at the time named the words appeared in red, with minute spots of blood. Surely we have here the explanation of the appearance of the "sacred stigmata" on ecstatic men and women meditating long on the passion of Christ.

Just as the body can be affected and the sense deceived, so can the inner sanctuary of the mind be invaded, and the will of the operator take the place of the paralysed volition of the subject. Then comes the possibility of suggesting action, action that may be either criminal or salutary. At the Salpêtrière and elsewhere suggestion of crime has been made and carried out after the subject has awaked; thus, told to poison one of the doctors with a glass containing water, the subject, after awaking, took the glass to him and offered him the water, with the remark that it was a hot day. Others have been made to stab one of the doctors present, to steal, *etc.*. [Binet and Féré, pp. 286-291] Considerable cunning is evinced in the way in which the suggestion is carried out so that the person under control becomes criminal of an especially dangerous type; the more so that the hypnotizer can at will destroy all memory alike of the suggestion and of the act. So serious to society has this new peril been considered, that both in Russia and Germany a law has been passed forbidding the practice of hypnotism by any but duly, authorized persons — a law which it is absolutely impossible to enforce.

On the other hand, suggestion may be used for the most beneficial purposes. At Nancy, Dr. Liébault and his colleagues have used it to promote moral action and to check criminal propensities; and, lately, the Rev. Mr. Tooth, of Croydon, has cured by suggestion confirmed dipsomaniacs. He suggests to them, while in the hypnotic trance, that drink is unpleasant to them, that it is nauseous and will make them sick; and in the waking state it has this effect upon them, so that they shrink from it with loathing. Truly there is here a mighty power for weal woe, according as it is used by pure or corrupt hands.

III - THE EXPLANATION

To the great majority of people the above facts are inexplicable, and it is noteworthy that the French experimenters offer no explanation of the facts they record. The explanation which I suggest, as a Theosophist, will be only a possible hypothesis for most of my readers, and will be promptly rejected by such of these as are Materialists.

We must now distinguish between Magnetism and Hypnotism, which, though closely allied by the phenomena they produce, are yet distinct in the agency employed. Animal Magnetism is, in its nature, nearly related to Mineral Magnetism, and is visible to the sensitive as light, as is the latter. Baron Reichenbach's famous researches proved that persons in a hyperaesthetic state could, when placed in a perfectly dark room, see a magnet by the luminosity surrounding it, a luminosity specially marked at the poles. ["*Physico-Physiological Researches in the Dynamic of Magnetism, etc., in their Relations to Vital Force*". Translated from the German by John Ashburner, M.D., Ed.. 1853] He found also that a similar luminosity is visible from the human hands, "brushes" being perceptible coming from the points of the fingers. This observation has been frequently repeated with clairvoyants, and the name of odyle, or odic force, has been given this human magnetism. The reality of this current from the body was curiously shown by the behaviour of a cat with Emma, Dr. Haddock's sensitive; the cat jumped on Emma's lap when she had been mesmerized, and she began to stroke its head with her right hand. "The cat instantly began to evince signs of fear or pain, and. to cry in a peculiar half- piteous, half-savage tone". The experiment was repeated with other cats and kittens, but some difficulty was experienced, "as the animals always became savage, and endeavoured to bite". When Emma was "away", *i.e.*, in the lucid somnambulic state, the left hand similarly affected the cat, showing that the currents in the body were reversed.[*Somnolism and Psychism*, pp. 109 -111]

No sign of any such current, or of the physical action of one human organism on another, has been observed in connection with hypnotism; a certain stimulus applied to the nerves seems to set up a bodily condition which is peculiarly sensitive to either internal or external stimuli; in the latter case the will of the operator comes in as the active agent.

There is little doubt that the ganglionic, or sympathetic, nervous system plays a great part in somnambulic phenomena, appearing indeed to act as the brain of the Sleep-Consciousness. In an account given in the *Lancet* [Vol. xxiii, pp. 663 *et seq.*] of an Italian woman who suffered from catalepsy, it is stated that the patient heard nothing by the ear, but "the lowest whisper directed on the hollow of the hand, or sole of the foot, on the pit of the stomach, or along the traject of "the sympathetic nerve", was perfectly heard. Mr. Colquhoun remarks "in many cases of catalepsy and somnambulism the usual organs of the senses have been found to be entirely dormant, and the seat of general sensibility transferred from the brain to the region of this ganglion, or *cerebrum abdominale*". [*Isis Revelata*, Vol. ii, p. 153] Du Prel remarks:

"Now, as waking consciousness proceeds parallel with corresponding changes of the senses and brain, so the transcendental psychological functions seem to be parallel with corresponding changes in the ganglionic system, whose central seat, the solar plexus, was already called by the ancients the seat of the belly. With a somnambule of the physician Petitin, the pit of the stomach protruded like a ball. Bertrand's somnambule said, pointing to her stomach, she had something there which spoke, and of which she could enquire....... A somnambule with Werner more particularly described the dualism of brain and solar plexus, as it reveals itself on the transition to somnambulism. Before her senses were suppressed, but while she was already gravitating towards somnambulism, she said: 'Where am I ?' I am not at home in the head. There is a strange struggle between the pit of the stomach and the head; both would prevail, both see and feel. That cannot be: it is a tearing asunder. It is as if I must send down the head into the stomach if I would see anything. The pit of the stomach pains me if I think above; and yet down there it is not clear enough. I must wonder, and that with the head, over the new disposition of the stomach". [*Philosophy of Mysticism*, vol. i, pp. 170.171]

It is held by many, and I think rightly, that the cerebrum is one pole of the human magnet, and the plexus solaris the other, although Reichenbach — from insufficient, data, as it seems to me — contended that this axis is only secondary, and that the primary axis transverse.

If we now examine the human consciousness, we shall find it broadly divided into two, the Sleeping and the Waking; all mesmeric, clairvoyant, hypnotic phenomena belong to the former, and the more complete the quiescence imposed on the bodily functions, the more vivid and intense are the activities of the "Sleep-Consciousness". One other point of grave significance should be noted: the hypnotized person on awaking knows nothing, save rarely, of what happened in the hypnotic trance; but "when he is asleep his memory embraces all the facts of his sleep, of his waking state, and of previous hypnotic sleeps. [Binet and Féré, p. 135] This Sleep - Consciousness, as seen at work in the somnambulic state, has a memory to which the waking memory is forgetfulness, can see in defiance of space and material obstruction, is keenly intellectual where the waking brain is dull, is to the Waking - Consciousness as a giant beside a dwarf. What is it, this luminous Eidolon which shines out the more brightly as the bodily frame is unconscious? I answer: it is the Inner Self, the true Individuality, the higher Ego, which dwells in the body as the flame in the lamp, sending into the outer world such shafts of its radiance as can pierce its covering.

This Consciousness of man is able to impress his physical brain and so become the Waking- Consciousness, just so far as physical conditions admit; what the Germans call the psycho-physical threshold divides, as it were, this Consciousness into two, not really dividing the Consciousness, but dividing off the amount it can impress on the physical organism from that which the physical organism is incapable of receiving. Of all that is below this threshold, the physical organism remains unconscious. The contents of the Waking - Consciousness are, then, only part of the contents of the Total Consciousness, and, indeed, a comparatively small part thereof. Now this threshold is variable, and varies with the physical condition; and the more sensitive the nervous system, the more outward stimuli are removed or the senses dulled to their reception, the more does this threshold sink, unveiling the contents of the Total, the Real Consciousness. So far the second class of phenomena is concerned, the exaltation of the senses and of the mental capacities, this hypothesis, worked out, will be found to be, thoroughly explanatory. Once realize that the physical organs of sense are, as has been well said, barriers between the inner senses, the perceptive faculties of the Inner Self, and the objective world, that they are *organs*, not faculties, and it will be seen how their paralysis may make way for the inner senses to function.

The third class of phenomena, the control of the individual by the operator, turns once more, as to the hallucinations, on this movability of the threshold of sensation. Let us conceive of existence as one vast line, which has spirit or force for one end and grossest matter for the other end, all phenomena, "material" and "immaterial", ranging between these not differing in essence, but in degree of condensation — so that condensed force would present itself as matter, rarefied matter as force. Let us consider, next, that the universe, to us, exists as conceived, our conception depending on the impression made by it on us through our senses. It will at once be seen that a thing will present itself to us as matter or as force according as it can or cannot affect our senses; that which affects the senses directly will be recognized as matter; that which is only apprehended by the mind through its effects will be recognized as force. Whether the mental presentment of a thing is material or immaterial will depend, then, on our sensibility and not on the thing itself, and the variation of our threshold of sensibility will transfer a thing from the matter-world to the force-world, and vice versa. [See the admirable argument on this subject in Du Prel's *Philosophy of Mysticism*. Vol. ii, pp. 130.135] Thus to our normal senses the attraction between the magnet and all iron within the magnetic field is invisible and we speak of the force of attraction: to the sensitive, or the somnambulist this force is visible as light. *The senses condition the nature of the perception.* Then, to abnormally sharpened senses, a thought may become a material object, force-vibrations becoming visible, *i.e.*, appearing as matter. But if this be so, the "hallucination" of the somnambulist, who sees a bird or a lamp-shade at the suggestion the hypnotizer, results from her threshold of sensibility being so shifted that the normally immaterial thought becomes to her material.

This hypothesis does not explain the paralysis of vision as to objects, or parts of objects, which is one of the most startling hypnotic phenomena. For elucidation of this I am somewhat at a loss. Patanjali speaks of the possibility of disconnecting "that property of Satwa which exhibits itself as luminousness" from the organ of sight of the spectator; [*Yoga Aphorisms*, Ed. 1889, p. 31] and the ancient Hindus held that there was this connection, so to speak, between the seer and the object seen. That an object *can* be made to disappear, I know, having seen it done and having been made myself to disappear; for the explanation, I am still groping. [*Vide* p. 24, *ante*; and *Invisible Helpers*, pp. 25, 26.. Ed.]

The control of acts is easier to understand, for here one can see that the Ego of the hypnotized person may, as it were, be thrust aside and the Ego of the hypnotizer take its place, using the brain and limbs of the subject as its tool. Be this as it may, the recognition of this true Ego, this Inner Self, acting in and through the body, but its master, not its product, offers, at least, a hopeful path to the solution of the abstruse problems that face us. That psychology should become in the West, as it is in the East, an experimental science, must be the wish of every patient searcher after Truth.

www.ingramcontent.com/pod-product-compliance
Lightning Source LLC
LaVergne TN
LVHW041459070426
835507LV00009B/696